First Facts®

easy origami

EASY ANIMAL Origami

by Christopher L. Harbo

CAPSTONE PRESS
a capstone imprint

First Facts is published by Capstone Press,
1710 Roe Crest Drive, North Mankato, Minnesota 56003.
www.capstonepub.com

Books published by Capstone Press are manufactured with paper
containing at least 10 percent post-consumer waste.

Library of Congress Cataloging-in-Publication Data
Harbo, Christopher L.
  Easy animal origami / by Christopher L. Harbo.
      p. cm.—(First facts. Easy origami)
  Includes bibliographical references.
  Summary: "Provides instructions and photo-illustrated diagrams for making a variety of easy animal
origami models"—Provided by publisher.
  ISBN 978-1-4296-5384-8 (library binding)
  1. Origami—Juvenile literature. 2. Animals in art—Juvenile literature. I. Title. II. Series.
  TT870.H3198 2011
  736'.982—dc22   2010024791

Editorial Credits
Designer: ALISON THIELE
Photo Studio Specialist: SARAH SCHUETTE
Scheduler: MARCY MORIN
Production Specialist: LAURA MANTHE

Photo Credits
Capstone Studio/Karon Dubke, all photos

Artistic Effects
Shutterstock/echo3005, michelleaanb, s26, valeriya_gold, Z-art

ABOUT THE AUTHOR

Christopher L. Harbo loves origami. He began folding
paper several years ago and hasn't quit since. In
addition to decorative origami, he also enjoys folding
paper airplanes. When he's not practicing origami,
Christopher spends his free time reading Japanese
comic books and watching movies.

Printed in the United States of America in North Mankato, Minnesota.
112011   006456R

TABLE OF
Contents

PAPER ZOO

Welcome to the origami zoo! As zookeeper, you'll turn paper squares into amazing animals. Tucked inside this book are seven of the easiest origami animals ever created. You'll fold a dog's head, a fluttering butterfly, a beautiful swan, and much more. Jump in and start folding your paper zoo!

MATERIALS

Origami is a simple art that doesn't use many materials. You'll only need the following things to complete the projects in this book:

Origami Paper: Square origami paper comes in many fun colors and sizes. You can buy this paper in most craft stores.

Letter-sized Paper: Not all origami models begin with a square. Use 8.5- by 11-inch (22- by 28-centimeter) paper when needed.

Ruler: Some models use measurements to complete. A ruler will help you measure.

Pencil: Use a pencil when you need to mark spots you measure with the ruler.

Craft Supplies: Markers and other craft supplies will help you decorate your models.

FOLDING TECHNIQUES

Folding paper is easier when you understand basic origami folds and symbols. Practice the folds on this list before trying the models in this book. Turn back to this list if you get stuck on a tricky step, or ask an adult for help.

Valley Folds are represented by a dashed line. One side of the paper is folded against the other like a book. A sharp fold is made by running your finger along the fold line.

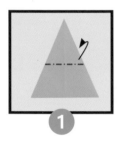

Mountain Folds are represented by a pink or white dashed and dotted line. The paper is folded sharply behind the model.

Squash Folds are formed by lifting one edge of a pocket. The pocket gets folded again so the spine gets flattened. The existing fold lines become new edges.

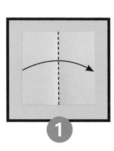
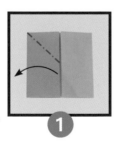

Inside reverse folds are made by opening a pocket slightly. Then you fold the model inside itself along existing fold lines.

6

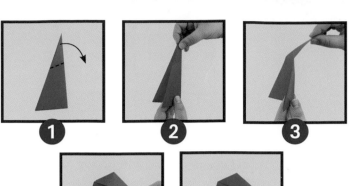

Outside reverse folds are made by opening a pocket slightly. Then you fold the model outside itself along existing fold lines.

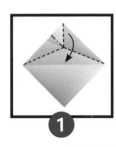

Rabbit ear folds are formed by bringing two edges of a point together using existing fold lines. The new point is folded to one side.

SYMBOLS

SINGLE-POINTED ARROW:
Fold the paper in the direction of the arrow.

HALF-POINTED ARROW:
Fold the paper behind.

DOUBLE-POINTED ARROW:
Fold the paper and then unfold it.

LOOPING ARROW:
Turn the paper over or turn it to a new position.

FLOPPY-EARED Dog

Traditional Model

Folding this paper dog is a snap! In only five simple steps you'll have a floppy-eared pup.

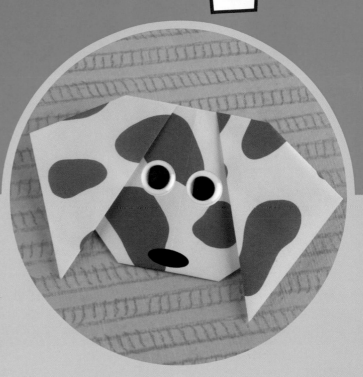

1

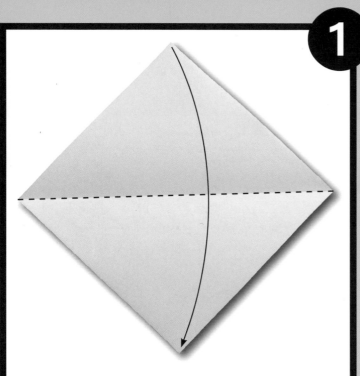

Start with the colored side of the paper face down. Valley fold the top point to the bottom point.

2

Valley fold the left point to the right point and unfold.

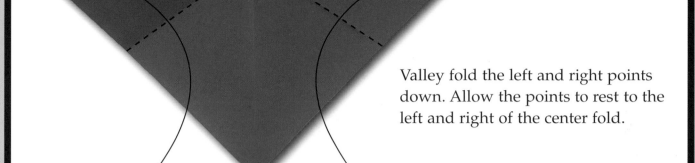

3

Valley fold the left and right points down. Allow the points to rest to the left and right of the center fold.

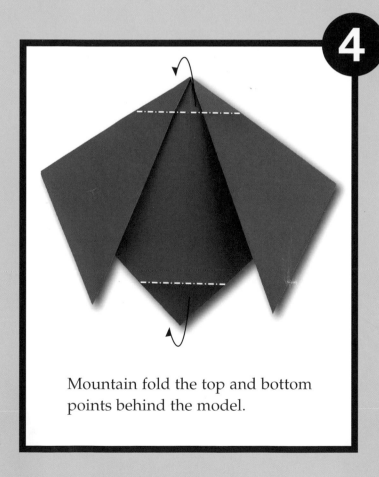

4

Mountain fold the top and bottom points behind the model.

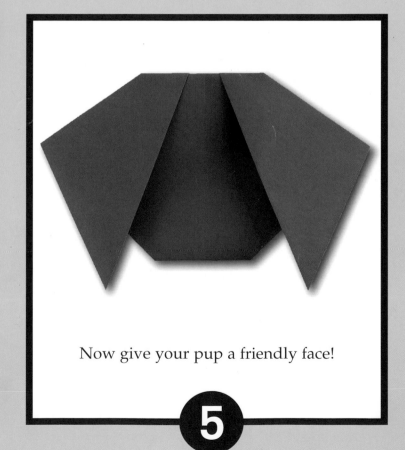

5

Now give your pup a friendly face!

SECRET Tip Let your pup's personality pop off the page with googly eyes and a pom-pom nose.

9

PURR-FECT Cat

Traditional Model

Some cats have tall, pointy ears. This cat copies those fancy features purr-fectly.

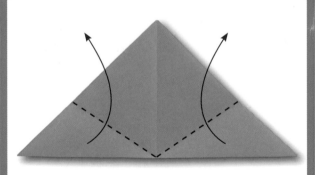

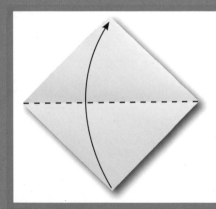

1

Start with the colored side of the paper face down. Valley fold the bottom point to the top point.

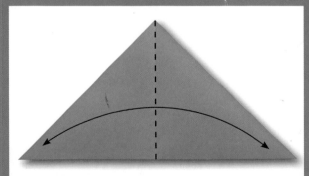

Valley fold the left point to the right point and unfold.

2

Valley fold the left and right points up. Allow the points to rest to the left and right of the center fold.

3

4

Valley fold the top point about halfway down the center fold.

5

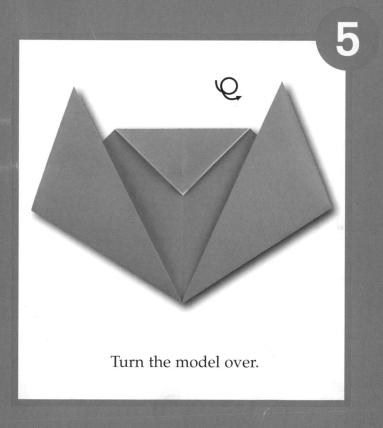

Turn the model over.

6

Add large eyes and a small nose to bring your cat to life.

SECRET Tip
Don't forget to add whiskers to your cat. Try using yarn or fishing line.

11

FLAPPING Butterfly

Traditional Model

Butterflies float through the air from flower to flower. This butterfly will amaze you with its graceful fluttering.

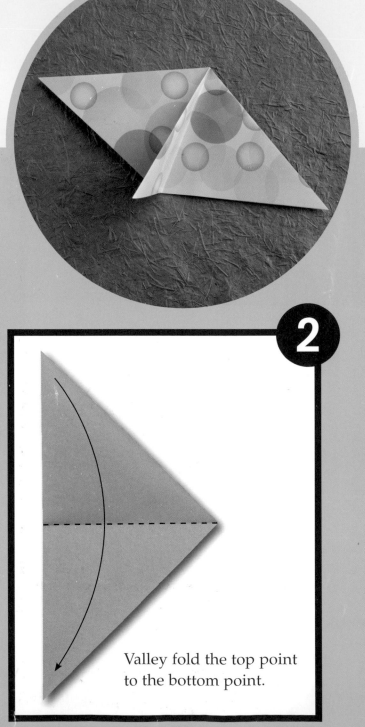

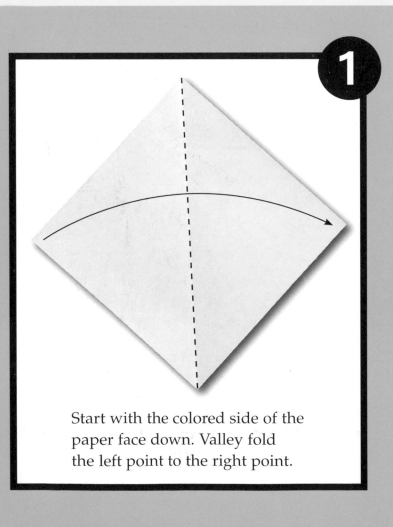

1

Start with the colored side of the paper face down. Valley fold the left point to the right point.

2

Valley fold the top point to the bottom point.

3

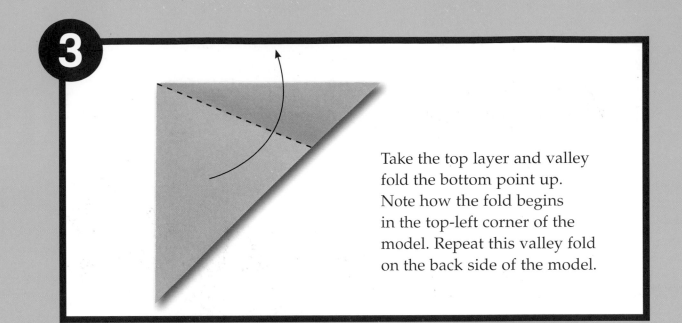

Take the top layer and valley fold the bottom point up. Note how the fold begins in the top-left corner of the model. Repeat this valley fold on the back side of the model.

4

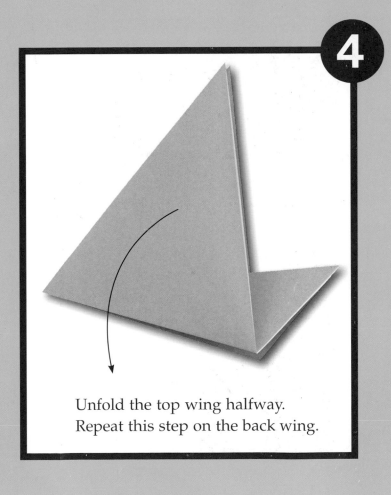

Unfold the top wing halfway. Repeat this step on the back wing.

Your butterfly is ready to fly. Press on its back to make the wings flutter.

5

SECRET Tip Curl the tips of your butterfly's wings up slightly with a pencil. Your butterfly is now an ocean stingray!

CROUCHING Bunny

Traditional Model

Rabbits crouch down in the grass when they eat. This folded bunny looks ready to nibble the top off a carrot.

1

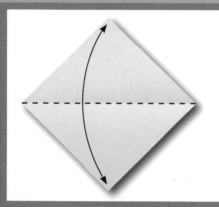

Start with the colored side of the paper face down. Valley fold the top point to bottom point and unfold.

2

Valley fold the top-left edge to the center fold. Valley fold the bottom-left edge to the center fold.

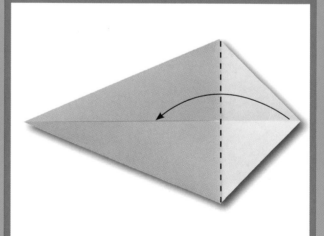

Valley fold the right point along the edge from step 2.

3

14

4

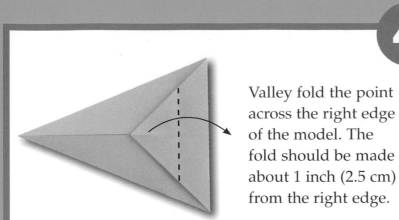

Valley fold the point across the right edge of the model. The fold should be made about 1 inch (2.5 cm) from the right edge.

5

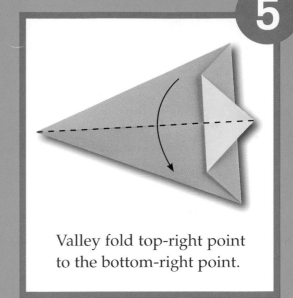

Valley fold top-right point to the bottom-right point.

6

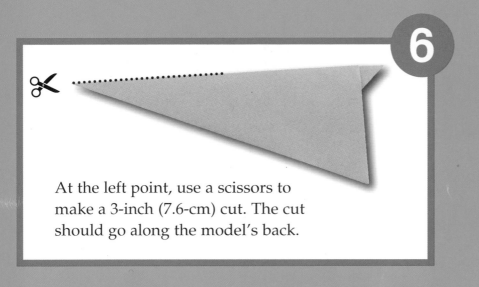

At the left point, use a scissors to make a 3-inch (7.6-cm) cut. The cut should go along the model's back.

7

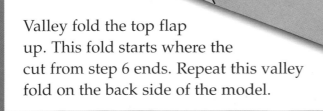

Valley fold the top flap up. This fold starts where the cut from step 6 ends. Repeat this valley fold on the back side of the model.

8

Help your bunny hop to the nearest carrot patch!

SECRET Tip

In step 7, fold the ears at slightly different angles. Doing so will help both ears show when the model is completed.

Spotted Ladybug

Traditional Model

Did you know ladybugs come in different colors? Use red paper to make the popular ladybug. Or use purple paper to make a ladybug that's all your own.

Start with the colored side of the paper face down. Valley fold the top point to the bottom point.

Valley fold the left point to the right point and unfold.

Valley fold the left and right points down. Allow the points to rest to the left and right of the center fold.

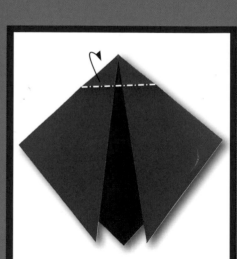

Mountain fold the top point behind the model.

5

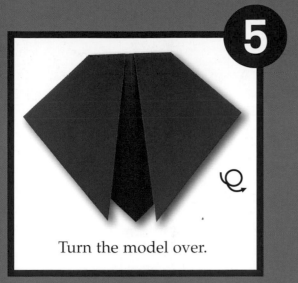

Turn the model over.

6

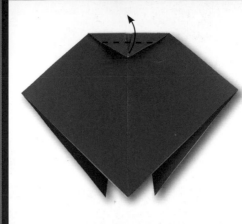

Valley fold the upside-down triangle at the top of the model. This fold is made about .25 inch (.64 cm) below the top edge. A smaller triangle will now stick out at the top.

7

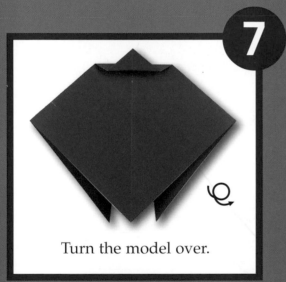

Turn the model over.

8

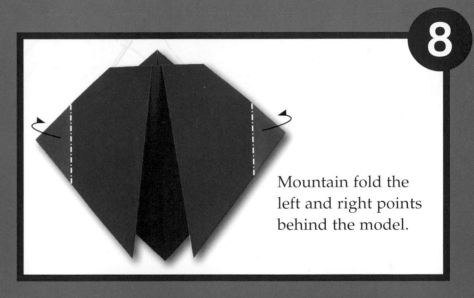

Mountain fold the left and right points behind the model.

9

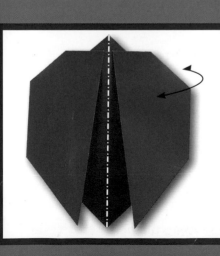

Mountain fold the right side of the model behind the left side and unfold.

10

Your ladybug is ready for spots. Draw them with a black marker.

SECRET

Tip

Curl the wings of your ladybug upward slightly to make the model look more lifelike.

PERCHED Parakeet

Are you looking for a paper pet that won't make a peep? This folded parakeet will keep you company without ever saying a word.

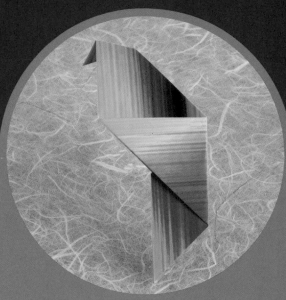

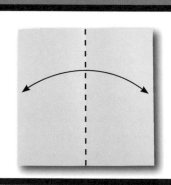

1 Start with the colored side of the paper face down. Valley fold the left edge to the right edge and unfold.

2 Valley fold the top-left corner to the center fold. Valley fold the top-right corner to the center fold.

3 Valley fold the left side to the center fold. Valley fold the right side to the center fold.

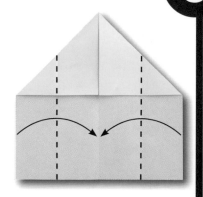

4 Mountain fold the right side of the model behind the left side.

5

Valley fold the bottom-right corner up and to the left. This fold begins on the right side of the model where another fold ends. After making a sharp fold, unfold the corner.

6

Reverse fold on the folds from step 5. This fold allows the bottom-right edge to swing up inside the model. When finished, a small square sticks out from the left side of the model.

7

Valley fold the top-left corner of the small square to the bottom-right corner.

8

Inside reverse fold on the folds from step 7. This fold allows the top-left corner to tuck inside the square.

9

Valley fold the top point to the left and unfold.

10

Inside reverse fold on the folds from step 9. This fold allows the point to stick out the left side of the model. Then turn the model slightly to the left.

11

Your parakeet looks ready to sit on your finger.

SWIMMING Swan

Traditional Model

Cranes, ducks, and other birds are popular origami models. This model uses both sides of the paper to form the royal swan.

1

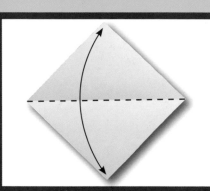

Start with the colored side of the paper face down. Valley fold the top point to the bottom point and unfold.

2

Valley fold the top-right edge to the center fold. Valley fold the bottom-right edge to the center fold.

3

Turn the model over.

4

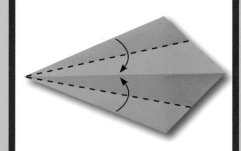

Valley fold the top-left edge to the center fold. Valley fold the bottom-left edge to the center fold.

5

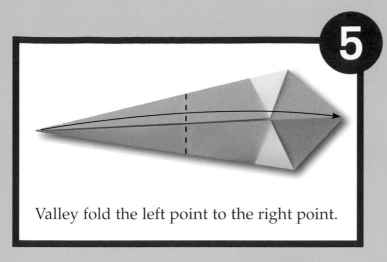

Valley fold the left point to the right point.

6

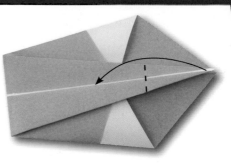

Valley fold the top layer's point to the center fold. Make this fold about 2 inches (5 cm) to the left of the point.

7

Mountain fold the top half of the model behind the bottom half.

8

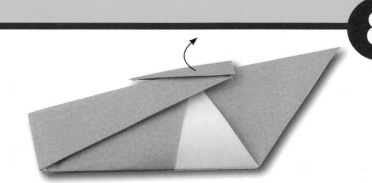

Pull the swan's beak up and to the right. The beak should point up and to the left. Press the swan's beak firmly to hold the folds in place.

9

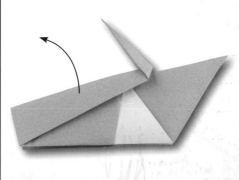

Pull the swan's neck up and to the left. When standing, the neck should point slightly to the right. Press the base of the neck to hold the folds in place.

10

Imagine your royal swan floating across a pond.

SECRET Tip Line up three small swans behind one large swan. They will look like three chicks following their mother.

Origami
PAPER PETS

READ More

Boonyadhistarn, Thiranut. *Origami: The Fun and Funky Art of Paper Folding.* Crafts. Mankato, Minn.: Capstone Press, 2007.

Boursin, Didier. *Folding for Fun.* Richmond Hill, Ont.: Firefly Books, 2007.

Engel, Peter. *10-Fold Origami: Fabulous Paperfolds You Can Make in 10 Steps or Less.* New York: Sterling Pub. Co., Inc., 2008.

Meinking, Mary. *Easy Origami.* Origami. Mankato, Minn.: Capstone Press, 2009.

INTERNET Sites

FactHound offers a safe, fun way to find Internet sites related to this book. All of the sites on FactHound have been researched by our staff.

Here's all you do:

Visit *www.facthound.com*

Type in this code: 9781429653848

Super-cool stuff! Check out projects, games and lots more at **www.capstonekids.com**